LUSIA HARRIS:
BASKETBALL STAR

NANCY LOEWEN

Text Copyright © 2025 Planting People Growing Justice Press
Illustrations copyright © 2025 Planting People Growing Justice Press

Cover Artwork and Illustrations by Whimsical Designs by CJ
Design by Reyhana Ismail

All rights reserved.

No part of this book may be reproduced in any manner without express written consent of the publisher, except in the case of brief excerpts in critical reviews and articles.

All inquiries or sales request should be addressed to:

Planting People Growing Justice Press
P.O. Box 131894
Saint Paul, MN 55113
www.ppgjli.org

Printed and bound in the United States of America
First Edition
LCCN: 2024951765
1-9781959223658/9798896050018-04/15/2025

DEDICATION

For Danette, who has helped so many children open doors.
For Veronica (Ronnie) Burton, educator and changemaker.

TABLE OF CONTENTS

Introduction
A Star Player 5

Chapter 1:
Long and Tall and That's Not All 9

Chapter 2:
A Game Changer 12

Chapter 3:
Mother, Teacher, Coach-and NBA Draft Pick 19

Chapter 4:
The Queen of Basketball 24

About the Author 27

Glossary 28

Source Notes, Books, Websites 30

Words in **bold** are in the glossary.

A STAR PLAYER

It's 1975. Two women's college basketball teams are competing for the national title. It's only the fourth time the tournament has been held. The Mighty Macs play for Immaculata University, a Catholic school in Pennsylvania. They've won the title three years in a row. Now they are playing the Lady Statesmen from Delta State University in Mississippi. Can the two-year-old Delta State team defeat the **reigning** champions?

As the players run back and forth on the court, the stadium fills with noise. Nuns bang on buckets. Everyone is shouting and cheering.

One player, the center from Delta State, stands out. She's 6' 3" and the only Black player, but that's not why all eyes are on her. She's clearly a star. With speed, strength, and grace, she drives, rebounds, blocks shots—and most of all, scores. Delta State fans are thrilled when she leads her team to a 90-81 victory.

Meet Lusia Harris, one of the all-time greats in women's basketball.

On the court, Harris was powerful. She was described as "**relentless**," "**dominant**," "unstoppable." But off the court, she was known for being humble and soft-spoken.

"I don't think I ever just sat down and said I was going to be an athlete," she once said. "I just played the game and always wanted to do my best."

FACT: AIAW

This championship game was part of the Association for Intercollegiate Athletics for Women (AIAW), which held national tournaments from 1972 to 1982.

After that, women's college sports became part of the National Collegiate Athletics Association (NCAA).

CHAPTER 1:
LONG AND TALL AND THAT'S NOT ALL

usia Harris (known as Lucy) was born on February 10, 1955, in Minter City, Mississippi. She had nine older brothers and sisters and one younger sister. Her parents were cotton farmers.

Growing up, Harris and her siblings worked hard. They picked cotton and grew vegetables. But they made time for fun, too. Harris loved playing backyard basketball with her brothers and neighbors.

Sometimes she stayed up past her bedtime to watch basketball on TV, muffling the sound with a quilt pulled over her head. She studied the moves of great NBA players such as Wilt Chamberlain and Oscar Robertson. Someday she would play like they did, she decided.

By the time Harris got to high school, she was 6' 3" tall. Kids sometimes teased her about her height. "Long and tall and that's all," they said. But they were wrong. At Amanda Elzy High School, Harris became a star basketball player. It wasn't always easy, though. Shooting the ball came naturally to her, but she had to learn how to play defense and offense.

Harris served as team captain, made the state All-Star team, and led the school to the state tournament. She was named the team MVP (most valuable player) three years in a row. She even set a school record by scoring 46 points in one game!

A GROUND-BREAKING EDUCATOR

The high school Harris attended was named after Amanda Belle Elzy. Elzy was an education **advocate**. She was probably the first Black assistant superintendent in the United States. In 1970, she was named Outstanding Educator of America.

CHAPTER 2:
A GAME CHANGER

Lusia Harris graduated from high school in 1973. She was set to go Alcorn State, a Black university, even though it didn't have a women's basketball team. Then she was asked to play for Delta State University in Cleveland, Mississippi. The coach, Margaret Wade, had been a star player there in the 1930s. The women's basketball program had ended years earlier. Now the school was bringing it back. Margaret Wade wanted to win. She wanted Harris on her team.

During her four years at Delta State, Harris was the only Black woman on the basketball team. She was one of very few Black students on campus. Delta State hadn't even accepted Black students until 1966.

Harris kept busy with classes, basketball practice, and games. She didn't become close friends with

AIMING FOR EQUALITY

Title IX is a 1972 law that bans sex **discrimination** in any educational program that receives funding from the **federal government**. Girls have to be given the same opportunities that boys are, from elementary school all the way through college. Women's sports took off dramatically when the law passed.

her Lady Statesmen teammates, but everyone got along. On the basketball court, all that mattered was the game.

In Harris's first season with Delta State, 1973–1974, the Lady Statesmen had a winning record but didn't make it to nationals. They were a brand-new team, after all. But in 1975, they beat the reigning champions, Immaculata University's Mighty Macs.

In 1976, they beat Immaculata again.

And in 1977, they beat Louisiana State University.

Three national championships in a row! Harris was a key player in all of them. She was named MVP all three years.

The success of the Lady Statesmen brought a lot of eager fans to women's college basketball. Harris herself had plenty of fans. In fact, she was so well-liked that she was voted homecoming queen in 1975.

In her later years, Harris was asked how playing for Delta State had influenced her. Surprisingly, her answer had little to do with basketball. "I think

I'm able to accept people just as they are because people accepted me just as I am," she said.

Besides playing for Delta State, Harris also played for the United States in other major tournaments. In 1975, she played in the world championships for FIBA, the international basketball **federation**. That year she also played in the Pan American Games, helping her team go undefeated to win the gold medal.

Then came the Olympics. The 1976 Summer Olympics in Montreal marked the first time women's basketball was played as an Olympic sport. In April that year, tryouts for the U.S. team were held in Tennessee. Hundreds of players competed for just a dozen spots on the team. Harris tried out—and made it.

In the very first game, the United States against Japan, Harris was the first player to score. "You just made history!" a teammate told her.

The U.S. team lost that game, but they went on to win the silver medal. Harris was an Olympic medalist.

COLLEGE CAREER STATS

109 games won; 6 games lost

2,981 points scored

1,662 rebounds

Averaged 25.9 points and 14.5 rebounds per game

Named to the All-American first team during Delta State's three winning seasons

CHAPTER 3:
MOTHER, TEACHER, COACH—AND NBA DRAFT PICK

The year after the Olympics, in 1977, Harris was invited to try out for the New Orleans Jazz basketball team. She'd been **drafted** by the NBA! (NBA stands for National Basketball Association.)

A 19-year-old named Denise Long had been chosen by the San Francisco Warriors in 1969. But the **league** hadn't allowed their pick. The Jazz's pick was allowed, making Harris the first woman to be officially drafted by the NBA.

Harris had her doubts about the offer. She didn't think she could compete with men, most of whom would be larger and stronger. Besides, she had entered another phase of her life. During her senior year at Delta State, she married her high school sweetheart, George E. Stewart. She wanted to start a family. She and her husband would eventually have four children: Christopher, Eddie, and twin daughters Christina and Crystal.

Later in her life, Harris was asked if she was sorry she'd turned down her chance to play for the NBA. She wasn't. She proudly listed the accomplishments of her children. All of them had earned advanced degrees. And all of them were athletes.

After college, Harris didn't have many options to keep playing basketball. She played for the Houston Angels in the Women's Professional Basketball League for one season, 1979–80. But the new league didn't last. It would be nearly 20 years before the WNBA (Women's National Basketball Association) would come along.

Still, basketball continued to shape Harris's life. She worked for Delta State as an **admissions** counselor and assistant basketball coach. Later she earned a master's degree in special education. She taught

FELLOW HALL OF FAMER

Like Harris, Cheryl Miller was in the first group of players inducted into the Women's Basketball Hall of Fame in 1999. She was a forward for the University of Southern California from 1982 to 1986. She led her team to several national championships. In 1984, she was a key player on the Olympic team that defeated the Soviets to win gold.

special education and coached basketball at the school where it all started, Amanda Elzy High School, and other area schools. Harris found that coaching basketball was harder than playing it. But she loved to see young players master new skills.

Harris never talked much about her basketball achievements. Her own children knew only bits and pieces of her story. They didn't realize the importance of her career until they were nearly grown.

In fact, Harris herself didn't truly understand what she'd accomplished until years later. At the time, she'd just been having fun playing basketball, traveling, and meeting people. But she came to realize that she and her teammates had done more than that. They had opened doors for other female athletes—both Black and white. Harris enjoyed watching women's basketball on television. It made her feel good to know that she'd helped those players get there.

CHAPTER 4:
THE QUEEN OF BASKETBALL

In later years, Harris paid a price for giving her all to the game. She had little **cartilage** left in her knees. When walking became too painful, she began using a wheelchair. She also suffered from **rheumatoid arthritis**, as well as a mental illness called **bipolar disorder**. But she handled these problems with the same approach that had served her so well in her basketball career. She just did her best.

In 2021, a short film shared Harris's story with the world. The Queen of Basketball was directed by award-winning filmmaker Ben Proudfoot. It won an **Academy Award** the following March.

Harris never knew about the award. She passed away on January 18, 2022, at the age of 66. Still, her last months were filled with good memories of those amazing years when she was at the top of her sport. In her modest way, she had broken barriers and created a lasting **legacy**.

FACT: MAKING HISTORY

1983: Delta State Sports Hall of Fame

1990: Mississippi Sports Hall of Fame

1992: Naismith Memorial Basketball Hall of Fame (Harris was the first female college player and the first Black woman to be inducted. She was escorted by her childhood idol, Oscar Robertson.)

1999: Women's Basketball Hall of Fame (Harris was in the inaugural class, along with coach Margaret Wade.)

2005: International Women's Sports Hall of Fame

After her death, praise for Harris came pouring in.

"A fierce competitor."

"She did what the team needed."

"She could outrebound everybody."

"The first truly dominant player of modern women's basketball."

"A record maker and record breaker."

"The world needs to know about her."

Lusia Harris's favorite saying was: "If you can dream it, you can do it."

As a Black girl growing up in a tiny town in Mississippi, she had dreamed of playing basketball like the NBA stars she watched on television.

And she'd done it.

ABOUT THE AUTHOR

Nancy Loewen grew up on a farm in southwestern Minnesota, surrounded by library books and cats.

She's published more than 140 books for children and young adults, including *The Everybody Club*, *Writer's Toolbox*, and *The LAST Day of Kindergarten* (a Minnesota Book Award finalist).

She lives in St. Paul.

GLOSSARY

Academy Award	Honors given each year to people with outstanding achievements in the movie industry. Winners receive small statues called Oscars
Admissions	In a school, the department that decides which students will be accepted
Advocate	A person who works to support a cause or group
Bipolar disorder	An illness that affects the brain and can cause intense mood swings
Cartilage	Tough tissue that is part of the skeleton. In people, it is found in the joints, ears, and nose
Discrimination	Treating certain groups of people unfairly because of wrong beliefs about who those people are
Dominant	The most powerful member or part of a group
Drafted	To be chosen by a professional sports team

Federal Government	The part of the United States government that deals with the entire country. Other governments are at the state, county, and city levels
Federation	A governing body that is formed when groups or clubs join together
League	In sports, a group of teams that play against one another on a regular basis.
Legacy	Something meaningful that is passed down from someone who went before.
Reigning	To rule or control; to be at the top.
Relentless	To keep going without stopping.
Rheumatoid arthritis	A disease that causes swelling and pain in the joints (the places where bones meet, such as elbows, knees, and hips).

SOURCE NOTES

"Interview with Lusia Harris, March 6, 2021." Louie B. Nunn Center for Oral History—Digital Exhibits. nunncenter.net/ohms-spokedb/render.php?cachefile=2021oh0151_ukabskw0010_ohm.xml.

Minta, Molly. "'Farewell Mother, Farewell My Queen': Family Remembers Lucy Harris in Emotional Ceremony." Mississippi Today, February 7, 2022. mississippitoday.org/2022/02/05/farewell-mother-farewell-my-queen-family-remembers-lucy-harris-in-emotional-ceremony.

Sandomir, Richard. "Lusia Harris, 'Queen of Basketball,' Dies at 66." The New York Times, January 20, 2022. nytimes.com/2022/01/20/sports/basketball/lusia-harris-dead.html.

The New York Times: The Learning Network . "Film Club: 'Almost Famous: The Queen of Basketball.'" The New York Times, February 10, 2022. nytimes.com/2022/02/10/learning/film-club-almost-famous-the-queen-of-basketball.html.

BOOKS

Davis, Amira Rose. (2024). *Go, Wilma, Go!: The Story of Wilma Rudolph's Fight Against Segregation.* Bloomsbury Children's Books.

Henderson, Leah. (2020). *Mamie on the Mound: A Woman in Baseball's Negro Leagues.* Capstone Editions.

Labrecque, Ellen. (2020). *The Story of the WNBA.* The Child's World.

WEBSITES

Bleacher Report
Lusia Harris: The First Woman Ever Drafted by an NBA Team—And Why She Turned Them Down (short video)
youtube.com/watch?v=dxcVmsvgfks

Kiddle
Lusia Harris Facts for Kids
kids.kiddle.co/Lusia_Harris

The Naismith Memorial Basketball Hall of Fame
Lusia Harris-Stewart
hoophall.com/hall-of-famers/lusia-harris-stewart

National Public Radio
Remembering legend Lusia Harris, the only woman to be officially drafted by the NBA
npr.org/2022/01/19/1074083938/lusia-harris-womens-basketball-nba-draft

ABOUT PLANTING PEOPLE GROWING JUSTICE LEADERSHIP INSTITUTE

Planting People Growing Justice Leadership Institute seeks to plant seeds of social change through education, training, and community outreach.

A portion of the proceeds from this book will support the educational programming of Planting People Growing Justice Leadership Institute.